Ecosystems

Rain Forests

by Nadia Higgins

Bullfrog Books

Ideas for Parents and Teachers

Bullfrog Books let children practice reading informational text at the earliest reading levels. Repetition, familiar words, and photo labels support early readers.

Before Reading

- Discuss the cover photo. What does it tell them?

- Look at the picture glossary together. Read and discuss the words.

Read the Book

- "Walk" through the book and look at the photos. Let the child ask questions. Point out the photo labels.

- Read the book to the child, or have him or her read independently.

After Reading

- Prompt the child to think more. Ask: Have you ever visited a rain forest? Have you seen videos or pictures? How would you describe it?

Bullfrog Books are published by Jump!
5357 Penn Avenue South
Minneapolis, MN 55419
www.jumplibrary.com

Library of Congress Cataloging-in-Publication Data

Names: Higgins, Nadia, author.
Title: Rain forests / by Nadia Higgins.
Description: Minneapolis, MN: Jump!, Inc., [2017]
Series: Ecosystems
Audience: Ages 5–8. | Audience: K to grade 3.
Includes bibliographical references and index.
Identifiers: LCCN 2016058423 (print)
LCCN 2016058904 (ebook)
ISBN 9781620316818 (hardcover: alk. paper)
ISBN 9781620317341 (pbk.)
ISBN 9781624965586 (ebook)
Subjects: LCSH: Rain forest ecology
Juvenile literature. | Rain forests—Juvenile literature.
Classification: LCC QH541.5.R27 H546 2017 (print)
LCC QH541.5.R27 (ebook) | DDC 577.34—dc23
LC record available at https://lccn.loc.gov/2016058423

Editor: Jenny Fretland VanVoorst
Book Designer: Molly Ballanger
Photo Researcher: Molly Ballanger

Photo Credits: Alamy: Anup Shah/naturepl.com, 10–11. Getty: Danita Delimont, 4; Ian Nichols, 5; Ippei Naoi, 12–13; Wolfgang Kaehler, 14; Bob Krist, 20–21. Shutterstock: Flame of life, cover; Dirk Ercken, 1; Kuttelvaserova Stuchelova, 3; Fernando Tatay, 6–7; Alan Kraft, 8; JIANG HONGYAN, 9; TJUKTJUK, 15; Jag-cz, 16–17; Rosa Jay, 17; Arten Samokhvalov, 18; duangnapa _ b, 18–19; worldswildlifewonders, 20–21; Alexander Mazurkevich, 24.

Printed in the United States of America at Corporate Graphics in North Mankato, Minnesota.

Table of Contents

Wet, Green, and Alive

A rain forest is a wet, green place.

Tall trees grow.

Rain falls almost every day.

Some rain forests are cool.

Earth's biggest trees grow here.

But most rain forests are hot.

The air is moist.

Plants love it!

A rain forest is
bursting with life.

Every space is filled.

Plants grow under
other plants.

They grow on top
of each other.

12

Many animals live high in the trees.

Monkeys swing.

Sloths hang.

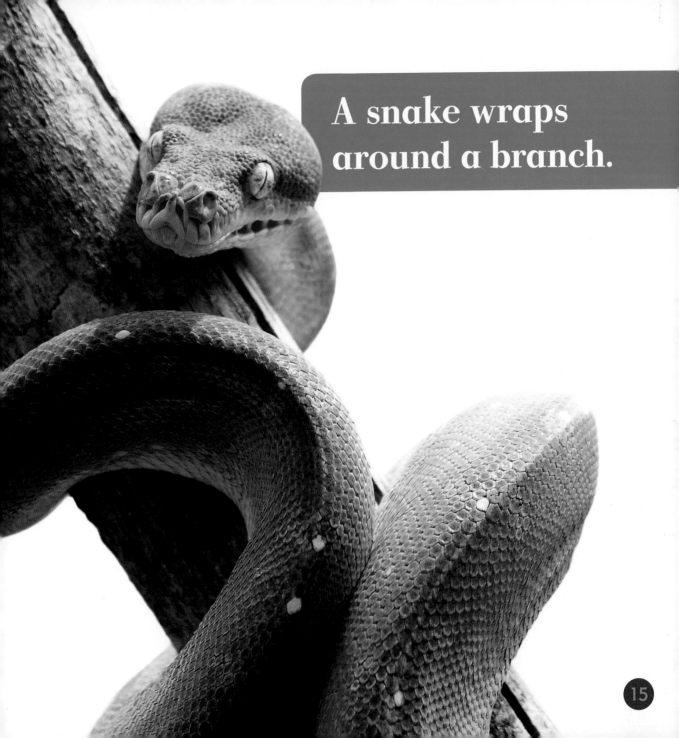

A snake wraps around a branch.

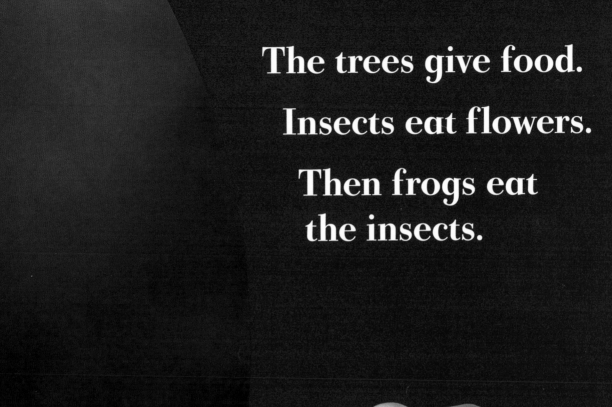

The trees give food.

Insects eat flowers.

Then frogs eat
the insects.

Birds eat fruit from trees.
That spreads seeds.

seeds

1043613

New trees will grow.

This wet, green
world lives on.

21

Where Are the Rain Forests?

The largest rain forest in the world grows around the Amazon River. It is mostly in the country of Brazil.

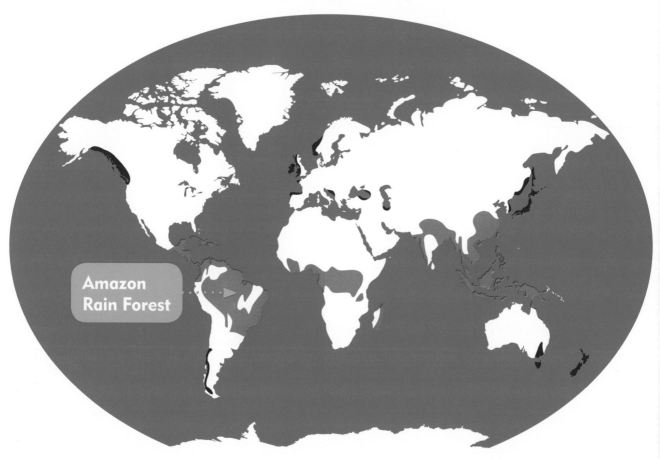

Amazon Rain Forest

◼ hot rain forest
◼ cool rain forest

Picture Glossary

insects
Small animals with six legs and three body parts.

seeds
The parts of a plant from which a new plant will grow.

moist
A little bit wet.

sloth
Furry mammals that move very slowly and hang from tree branches in the rain forest.

Index

To Learn More

Learning more is as easy as 1, 2, 3.

1) Go to www.factsurfer.com

2) Enter "rainforests" into the search box.

3) Click the "Surf" button to see a list of websites.

With factsurfer.com, finding more information is just a click away.